Little Angels

Dealing With The Loss and Grief of A Miscarriage

And

Life After Loss

LITTLE ANGELS: DEALING WITH THE LOSS AND GRIEF OF MISCARRIAGE AND LIFE AFTER LOSS

First edition. November 13, 2023.

Copyright © 2023 Maria Davis.

ISBN: 979-8223187363

Written by Maria Davis.

Table of Contents

To my baby, who lived a perfect life.

To my husband, who loves me.

To God, who will always hold me.

Maria Davis

2023

2 Samuel 12:21-23

His advisers were amazed. "We don't understand you," they told him. "While the child was still living, you wept and refused to eat. But now that the child is dead, you have stopped your mourning and are eating again."

David replied, "I fasted and wept while the child was alive, for I said, 'Perhaps the Lord will be gracious to me and let the child live.' But why should I fast when he is dead? Can I bring him back again? I will go to him one day, but he cannot return to me."

Little Angels: Dealing With The Loss and Grief of A Miscarriage

Introduction

I'm sorry.

That pain you are feeling right now makes you feel like you're drowning. It's as if the sun has completely vanished from your life.

Where do you go from here?

Everyone experiences pain and grief differently. However different, I do understand the hollowness that's consuming you right now. I still remember everything like it happened yesterday.

My first appointment was on March 30th, nine weeks pregnant and absolutely elated at what the future held. My thoughts danced around the sound of my baby's heartbeat, the sound of their laughter, and all the memories we would create together. How could I not fall in love with this small bundle growing inside of me? However, during the ultrasound, the doctor realized my baby had stopped growing at six weeks- I had a missed miscarriage.

It was as if the floor disappeared from beneath me.

Where do I go from here?

I went home that day, a different person. The grief was all consuming and I thought at any moment the world was going to implode. How do you come back from this? I vaguely remembered my doctor laying out the different options I could take if I was unable to pass the baby on my own.

I prayed and I prayed *hard* that somehow this was a mistake, that somehow the technician messed up and I was still carrying a healthy baby in my womb. After a week, it was time for my follow-up appointment. I remember walking into the ultrasound room trembling. However, as I laid there watching the large screen in front of me, I realized that it was the best thing that could have ever happened to me.

Because as the technician moved the ultrasound, it caught the most beautiful thing.

2

A flicker.

A small heart beat.

It showed my little baby only registering at 6 weeks and 3 days but on that screen, I could see the little heartbeat flicker as if saying:

"Mommy, I'm right here! Can't you see me?"

At ten weeks pregnant, my little one was only showing to be six weeks and three days. The technician stared at the screen unsure of what to say. What could you say? However, that sweet little heartbeat flickered slowly and I knew then that God had given me the chance to say goodbye to my baby one last time. The next day, he or she would be gone.

Despite the pain, grief, and confusion, I can say that: you will see the light again; one day, you're going to smile and feel whole once more.

The pain will get easier.

After my miscarriage, I often wondered what was the purpose of all this. I was constantly asking God for guidance and understanding; I needed help with my sorrow and confusion. Where was he? Does he hear me? Was I alone in this?

Eventually, God *did* answer.

I had been reading previous bible study notes when He placed it in my heart to share His Word with you. That day felt so dark as I prayed for his guiding hand to lead me-and he *did*. God gave me the desire to read my past notes. In them, I found his voice and He answered me.

I hope this small bible study helps you as it did me.

After I came to terms that my baby wasn't going to make it, I told God and my husband this one thing and I hope it helps you.

"Seven months from now I was supposed to hold my baby; instead, I'll have to wait a little longer until God calls me home."

Our babies are still living and they are patiently waiting for us. We haven't nor will we ever lose them. The pain is real but so is our God. Lean on Him with all your heart and He will carry you.

Notes on the S.O.A.P. Method of Bible Study

This bible study uses the S.O.A.P. method. Please grab a notebook to journal your thoughts as you read through the study.

S.O.A.P. is a simple method for reading and applying God's word to our lives.

SOAP stands for Scripture, Observation, Application, and Prayer in four easy steps:

Scripture – Read a Bible verse out loud, and write it out.

Observation – What is the main message of the verse? What thoughts, words, or ideas stand out to you?

Application – Ask God how to apply the verse to your life.

Prayer – Pray God's Word back to him. Thank him for the revelations his Word brings you.

Day One

Job 8:21

"He will once again fill your mouth with laughter and your lips with joy."

I know it's hard to comprehend that something so little as laughing can seem like a distant dream. Mourning is a natural response but we have to remember that one day God is going to give us that desire to laugh and smile again.

One day, you'll realize that the heartache isn't all-consuming and the tears aren't as frequent.

One day, you're going to wake up and not feel forgotten or abandoned.

One day, you're going to realize that it was God breathing new life into you.

This verse has stayed with me through my darkest days. Even now, when the good days outweigh the bad, I keep this verse close to my heart as a reminder of God's promise to me.

A reminder that pain and suffering do not last forever.

Grab your journal and write Job 8:21

What did you observe? How can you apply Job 8:21 to your life? Most importantly, what will you're Prayer be?

Day Two

Romans 8:35

"Can anything ever separate us from Christ's love? Does it mean he no longer loves us if we have troubles or calamity, or are persecuted, or hungry, or destitute, or in danger, or threatened with death?"

I couldn't count how often I felt alone as I prayed to God for understanding. For days on end, I would seek God's answer to only be met with silence.

Where was he? Where was the Lord Almighty?

My heart was shattered and yet I refused to let that control me. With every part of me; I threw myself at the Lord's feet, I clung to him as though I was the one dying, and through that, he gave me strength.

How could I ever wonder if there was any chance that God could abandon me? God sent his own son to die on the cross for me. God's love is *eternal!* He will never leave us alone, especially in the midst of our despair.

Grab your journal and write Romans 8:35

What did you observe? How can you apply Romans 8:35 to your life? Most importantly, what will you're Prayer be?

Day Three

"He went on a little farther and bowed with his face to the ground, praying, "My Father! If it is possible, let this cup of suffering be taken away from me. Yet, I want your will to be done, not mine."

No one likes to suffer. Including *Jesus*.

On the night Jesus prayed he knew what his future held, the type of suffering he was about to endure and he asked God to take his *"cup of suffering "* away.

Jesus knew what was at stake; and although he was terrified, Jesus surrendered himself to the Lord's will.

Shouldn't we have that same mindset? When things are terrifying and all-consuming, shouldn't we pray, *"What is your purpose, Lord? Help guide me so that I can better serve you. Give me the strength and peace that I need Lord so that your will be done. In Jesus' name, amen."*

There were times in my past when I fought God out of fear, I was never able to surrender myself to the Lord and accept his will. At the end of the day, what did I accomplish? Absolutely nothing.

I changed nothing in the end.

After I was able to see my little baby's heartbeat, I realized that in order to have peace I had to give myself fully to the Lord, not only that but the baby as well.

Grab your journal and write Matthew 26:39

What did you observe? How can you apply Matthew 26:39 to your life? Most importantly, what will you're Prayer be?

Day Four

Psalms 34:17-18

"The Lord hears his people when they call to him for help. He rescues them from all their troubles. The Lord is close to the broken hearted; he rescues those whose spirits are crushed."

The Lord hears us when we cry out to him. Or, the sigh that leaves our lips when no words can be formed. God *sees* us and he sees the pain in our broken hearts. There were times when I thought I was alone but I was wrong.

Looking back now, I'm able to see all the times God has been there for me. Cling to this reminder as I have. Cling to it and know that God will rescue you, he hears you, and he is with you.

Grab your journal and write Psalm 34:17-18

What did you observe? How can you apply Psalm 34:17-18 to your life? Most importantly, what will you're Prayer be?

Day Five

Psalm 147:3

"He heals the brokenhearted and bandages their wounds."

One day the Lord will once again fill your mouth with laughter and your lips with joy according to *Job 8:21*.

Take comfort in knowing God is not only going to mend your wounds but he is also going to heal them. With time, the pain will start to ease and you'll be able to think of your little angel and smile without any tears.

Right now, allow our Lord to heal you. Lay at his feet so that he can mend your wounds and heal your broken heart. Praise him through the storm.

Praise him because after this storm there is always a rainbow waiting to be seen.

Grab your journal and write Psalm 147:3

What did you observe? How can you apply Psalm 147:3 to your life? Most importantly, what will you're Prayer be?

Day Six

Isaiah 40:31

"But those who trust in the Lord will find new strength. They will soar high on wings like eagles. They will run and not grow weary. They will walk and not faint."

Days, weeks, months, even years later we are going to look back one day and realize that the God who created the universe gave *you* the strength to carry on. It wasn't until several weeks after my miscarriage that I realized this.

My emotions were on a perpetual rollercoaster ride, up was down, and left was right and yet somehow, I still found the strength to pray. To keep moving even though all I wanted was my baby.

God will give you the strength to get through today and tomorrow, he loves you!

Grab your journal and write Isaiah 40:31

What did you observe? How can you apply Isaiah 40:31 to your life? Most importantly, what will you're Prayer be?

Day Seven

Isaiah 60:20

"Your sun will never set; your moon will not go down. For the Lord will be your everlasting light. Your days of mourning will come to an end."

Life will always be in a constant state of change; the seasons, people, including our emotions. The one thing that remains true is our Lord and his love for us. In him, his love will always be constant, he rescues those who are crushed and he promises that our days of mourning will come to an end.

When I first discovered this verse, a flower of hope blossomed in me, *my days of mourning will come to an end.* There will be a day when my heart will no longer ache.

Pray to God and let his everlasting light envelope you.

Grab your journal and write Isaiah 60:20

What did you observe? How can you apply Isaiah 60:20 to your life? Most importantly, what will you're Prayer be?

Day Eight

John 16:33

"I have told you all this so that you may have peace in me. Here on earth you will have many trials and sorrows. But take heart, because I have overcome the world."

In *John 16:33*, Jesus reminds us to have peace in him. In this life, we will face many trials and sorrow but he wanted to make one thing clear: *He has overcome the world.*

Before you and I were formed, God knew the heartache we were going to face, he knew the trials and wanted to remind us that all will be well.

At the beginning of my miscarriage, when I could not fathom the idea of losing my sweet baby, I kept wondering why?

Why me? Why my baby? Why? Why? Why?

No one is excluded from suffering, that is the whole point of this passage but Jesus made sure to announce it to everyone so that we would not get stuck on the bad things.

I could not imagine that one day I would find peace, but here I am. The good days are beginning to outweigh the bad and the tears are becoming less frequent.

Keep hanging on.

Grab your journal and write John 16:33

What did you observe? How can you apply John 16:33 to your life? Most importantly, what will you're Prayer be?

Day Nine

Deuteronomy 31:6

"So be strong and courageous! Do not be afraid and do not panic before them. For the Lord your God will personally go ahead of you. He will neither fail you nor abandon you.
"

When you are in the eye of the storm and everything is falling apart, it is easy to become terrified and hopeless. When the thought of miscarriage crossed my doctor's mind it devastated me. However, it was nothing compared to what I felt when it finally did occur.

My world which had been so bright was suddenly dark. *Where do I go from here?*

The thought of trying again hurt just as bad because I felt like we were replacing the baby we lost. It was absolutely devastating.

There are good and bad days and it is on those days where my heart can't seem to heal that God whispers this verse to me.

Through it all, God has been with me; protecting me from things seen and unseen. He sat with me as I cried. He sat with me as I obsessed over the *what if's,* he's been with me through it all. Quietly reassuring me that everything will be okay; quietly giving me the strength to go on with life; and quietly giving me the courage to try again.

Cling to him with all your heart and give all of your pain to him. Don't let your pain consume you.

Instead, relish in the strength and courage that the Lord has given you and keep fighting.

Grab your journal and write Deuteronomy 31:6

What did you observe? How can you apply Deuteronomy 31:6 to your life? Most importantly, what will you're Prayer be?

Day Ten

Revelation 21:4

"He will wipe every tear from their eyes, and there will be no more death or sorrow or crying or pain. All these things are gone forever. "

Do you remember how Jesus states that he has overcome the world in *John 16:33*?

One day death, sorrow, and pain will be a distant memory.

One day our tears will dry up and be no more.

One day, we are going to see our loved ones again and there will be nothing but happiness.

One day, I'm going to see my little angel again and so will you.

One day.

Until then, allow God to wipe away your tears. Allow him to hold you and mend your broken pieces back together. Give it all to him.

Grab your journal and write Revelation 21:4

What did you observe? How can you apply Revelation 21:4 to your life? Most importantly, what will you're Prayer be?

Day Eleven

Psalm 4:7

"You have given me greater joy than those who have abundant harvests of grain and new wine."

Once I realized that my baby was no longer with me, a part of me died. I couldn't understand why God would allow me to experience this precious moment just for me to lose it. Despite the confusion, I clung to his word. And in his word is where I found hope again.

Yes, my baby is no longer with me but he or she is home with the Lord. Because of this, my baby and yours will never know what grief is or what it means to suffer- our babies are at home with the Lord!

Realizing this has helped me so much over my journey with grief. Yes, I still miss my baby and there are days where I pray that things were different. Ultimately, it is the Lord's will, there was a purpose for calling my baby back home. In it, the Lord protected me and he protected my baby. Why wouldn't I sing praises of joy knowing that God-*the author of creation-* has everything in control?

Grab your journal and write Psalm 4:7

What did you observe? How can you apply Psalm 4:7 to your life? Most importantly, what will you're Prayer be?

Day Twelve

Romans 15:13

"I pray that God, the source of hope, will fill you completely with joy and peace because you trust in him. Then you will overflow with confident hope through the power of the Holy Spirit."

Lastly, I thought this verse would be the perfect ending to this Bible study. Let God's love consume you, let your faith in him consume you. Let everything about our Lord consume you.

Through it all, even in our valley of death, God stood beside us and in front of us. In our moments of weakness, it was God who gave us the strength to keep going.

There will be dark days ahead, we know this because of *John 16:33*, but Jesus has conquered the world. Don't let the grief consume you.

Instead, allow God's faithfulness to take control. Believe in him and you will live.

Grab your journal and write Romans 15:13

What did you observe? How can you apply Romans 15:13 to your life? Most importantly, what will you're Prayer be?

God has you in his arms, I have you in my heart.

Little Angels Book 2: Life After Loss
Introduction

Hey there,

If you're reading this then I know you're struggling.

You're struggling with what today might hold or a year from now, you're struggling to get past the next few seconds because your heart is pounding and you feel as though you can't breathe.

As a child of God, you've forgotten who you are.

The journey that I have been on after losing my baby has not been easy. It has been gut-wrenching and sometimes soul-crushing. However, as Jesus leaned onto his father at Gethsemane, so will we in our pain and suffering.

Several months after the miscarriage, I thought I was getting better but then the anxiety and fear of the future slowly started to trickle its way in.

Fear of losing someone else that I love.

Fear of the current worldly events.

Pain over my baby.

Fear of not being able to conceive again.

Before I realized what was happening, my world was beginning to tilt yet again.

Where do I go from here?

If you're hurting or if you feel stuck, I *understand*. However, please know that this is not where our story ends- far from it!

With this second half of the Bible study, I hope to challenge you, encourage you; and lastly, give you hope as you go through your next battle of *Life After Loss*.

Day One

Psalm 56:3

"But when I am afraid, I will put my trust in you. I praise God for what he has promised. I trust in God, so why should I be afraid? What can mere mortals do to me?"

The thoughts started in small waves but soon grew into something more.

"What if I lose another baby?"

"What if I lose someone that I love?"

"What if...?"

I began to obsess over Every. Little. Thing.

The thoughts plagued me in my quiet moments, and it felt like I was drowning all over again- *how long will this last?*

However, it was in these quiet moments, where my thoughts waged war against me that I discovered God's goodness, once again.

"When I am afraid, I put my trust in you..."

In that moment, I wasn't cured but it felt like someone had breathed new life into me. The elephant that sat on my chest was no longer there; slowly, I began to remember all of God's goodness. And, although, I wasn't cured in that moment, it was a corner stone that I desperately needed.

Since then, I've kept all of Psalm 56 close to me. My heart which was so heavy with fear and anxiety, slowly became lighter.

Instead of focusing on the fear and anxiety... why not put your trust in the Lord who created you?

What did you observe? How can you apply Psalm 56:3 to your life? Most importantly, what will you're Prayer be?

Day Two

Psalm 31:24

"So be strong and courageous, all you who put your hope in the Lord!"

I remember the first time someone told me to be strong. They meant well and were hoping to encourage me but all I felt was dread.

The mere thought of being strong felt so daunting- it seemed impossible to do.

How could I be strong when everything else felt so brittle? It was an endless cycle with no way to escape.

I didn't realize it then but the Lord was giving me the strength to get through the next day.

"One step at a time," He'd whisper, ever so gently.

That's all he requires is for us to take that next step and He will do the rest.

What did you observe? How can you apply Psalm 31:24 to your life? Most importantly, what will you're Prayer be?

Day Three

Psalm 42:1-11

"As the deer longs for streams of water, so I long for you, O God. I thirst for God, the living God.

When can I go and stand before him? Day and night I have only tears for food, while my enemies continually taunt me, saying,

"Where is this God of yours?"

My heart is breaking as I remember how it used to be: I walked among the crowds of worshipers, leading a great procession to the house of God, singing for joy and giving thanks amid the sound of a great celebration!

Why am I discouraged? Why is my heart so sad?

I will put my hope in God! I will praise him again— my Savior and my God!

Now I am deeply discouraged, but I will remember you— even from distant Mount Hermon, the source of the Jordan, from the land of Mount Mizar.

I hear the tumult of the raging seas as your waves and surging tides sweep over me. But each day the Lord pours his unfailing love upon me, and through each night I sing his songs, praying to God who gives me life.

"O God my rock," I cry, "why have you forgotten me? Why must I wander around in grief, oppressed by my enemies?"

Their taunts break my bones. They scoff, "Where is this God of yours?"

Why am I discouraged? Why is my heart so sad? I will put my hope in God! I will praise him again— my Savior and my God!"

Having anxiety, depression, or both can be so isolating. The author of this Psalm knew exactly that. He poured his heart out to the Lord because he felt alone; he doesn't understand why his soul is so downcast or why his enemies (our thoughts) are taunting him. All he knew to do was cry out to the Lord for help.

God hears our cries for help! He is close to the brokenhearted, and yet... we often forget this. We forget because in our fear, in our anxiety, the devil attacks us with his lies.

How do we remember God's promise? By remembering John 14:27, *"Peace I leave with you; my peace I give you."*

Rest in Him with all your heart!

What did you observe? How can you apply Psalm 42:1-11 to your life? Most importantly, what will you're Prayer be?

Day Four

Deuteronomy 31:8

"Do not be afraid or discouraged, for the Lord will personally go ahead of you. He will be with you; he will neither fail you nor abandon you."

Life moves on, but how do you?

There were times where I felt stuck. People were moving on with their lives; and here I was, afraid to take that next step. Still, as I began to discover verses such as *Psalm 56:3* or *John 16:33*, it became clear just how wonderful our Lord is. Yes, we may not understand his ways, but we can trust wholeheartedly that He will go before us and walk beside us because of His *love*.

As you begin to read your Bible, search for *Mathew 6:8* and keep it tucked inside your heart.

"Your Father knows what you need before you ask Him."

<u>*Hang in there.*</u>

What did you observe? How can you apply Deuteronomy 31:8 to your life? Most importantly, what will you're Prayer be?

Day Five

2 Corinthians 4:16-18

"That is why we never give up. Though our bodies are dying, our spirits are being renewed every day.

For our present troubles are small and won't last very long. Yet they produce for us a glory that vastly outweighs them and will last forever!

So we don't look at the troubles we can see now; rather, we fix our gaze on things that cannot be seen. For the things we see now will soon be gone, but the things we cannot see will last forever."

Each day that God sits with us, He breathes new life into our lungs. In our pain, we don't realize that God has his loving hands on us- *urging* our broken pieces back together. Oftentimes, when we are consumed by our grief and pain we forget that it's only temporary.

Our time here is temporary.

Our *pain* is temporary.

At the end of the day, we know that God loves us. We know that at the end of our journey, God is going to take us home.

Keep your eyes fixed on what you can not see. Seek the Lord with all your might, remind your heart of his promises, and the home that awaits us.

What did you observe? How can you apply 2 Corinthians 4:16-18 to your life? Most importantly, what will you're Prayer be?

Bonus Chapter

Genesis 18:1-5

Sarah

The Lord appeared again to Abraham near the oak grove belonging to Mamre.

One day Abraham was sitting at the entrance to his tent during the hottest part of the day. He looked up and noticed three men standing nearby. When he saw them, he ran to meet them and welcomed them, bowing low to the ground. "My Lord," he said, "if it pleases you, stop here for a while. Rest in the shade of this tree while water is brought to wash your feet. And since you've honored your servant with this visit, let me prepare some food to refresh you before you continue on your journey."

"All right," they said. "Do as you have said."

So Abraham ran back to the tent and said to Sarah, "Hurry! Get three large measures of your best flour, knead it into dough, and bake some bread."

Then Abraham ran out to the herd and chose a tender calf and gave it to his servant, who quickly prepared it. When the food was ready, Abraham took some yogurt and milk and the roasted meat, and he served it to the men. As they ate, Abraham waited on them in the shade of the trees.

"Where is Sarah, your wife?" the visitors asked.

"She's inside the tent," Abraham replied.

Then one of them said, "I will return to you about this time next year, and your wife, Sarah, will have a son!"

Sarah was listening to this conversation from the tent. Abraham and Sarah were both very old by this time, and Sarah was long past the age of having children. So she laughed silently to herself and said,

"How could a worn-out woman like me enjoy such pleasure, especially when my master—my husband—is also so old?"

Then the Lord said to Abraham, "Why did Sarah laugh? Why did she say, 'Can an old woman like me have a baby?' Is anything too hard for the Lord? I will return about this time next year, and Sarah will have a son."

Sarah was afraid, so she denied it, saying, "I didn't laugh." But the Lord said, "No, you did laugh."

Day Six

Romans 8:26-27

"And the Holy Spirit helps us in our weakness.

For example, we don't know what God wants us to pray for. But the Holy Spirit prays for us with groanings that cannot be expressed in words. And the Father who knows all hearts knows what the Spirit is saying, for the Spirit pleads for us believers in harmony with God's own will."

There were so many times when I wanted to pray but nothing came to mind. All I knew was that my heart was shattered, my soul was exhausted, and my mind was lost.

There were so many things I wanted to say and yet nothing at all.

Little did I know, that the whole time, the Holy Spirit was intercepting on my behalf.

Speaking to the God who loves me, what I needed before realizing that I needed it.

On those days, when words escape you, it's okay. You have someone speaking on your behalf!

You are never alone even when everything is falling apart on the inside and life is moving on. The Holy Spirit is speaking for you and God is beside you.

What did you observe? How can you apply Romans 8:26-27 to your life? Most importantly, what will you're Prayer be?

Day Seven

Lamentations 3:31-32

"For no one is abandoned by the Lord forever. Though he brings grief, he also shows compassion because of the greatness of his unfailing love."

Lamentations 3:31-32 is another great reminder that God -the creator of the universe- is always with you.

Jesus told us in *John 16:33* that we will have struggles.

Being alive means that you will experience pain, but it also means that we will experience unbelievable joy from the one who formed us.

Pain gives birth to joy and it took me a long time to realize that. Once I began to see that light at the end of the tunnel, all of God's blessings became evident in my life.

I'm saved, my little family loves me, I'm not who I once was.

My life is not the same and I'm glad it isn't. God's love is what got me through my darkest moments. It was his love that moved through my husband to take care of me.

Even if you can't see or feel it, He's taking care of you too.

What did you observe? How can you apply Lamentations 3:31-32 to your life? Most importantly, what will you're Prayer be?

Day Eight

Isaiah 41:10

"Don't be afraid, for I am with you. Don't be discouraged, for I am your God. I will strengthen you and help you. I will hold you up with my victorious right hand."

On the days when your thoughts wage war against you- remember this verse.

When your heart is thumping hard against your chest and the air escapes your lungs, remember that God will take care of you.

Experiencing emotions is normal; just as the seasons change, so will we. That's why in *Proverbs 3:5*, it states: *"Trust in the Lord with all your heart; do not depend on your own understanding."*

Give your fear to the Lord and all of the anxiety and intrusive thoughts that come along with it. Don't stay in that dark place, you weren't meant to live there! Our God is a mighty God and He will sustain you.

We may not realize it now but eventually, that fear of what the future might hold will slowly start to seep away.

What did you observe? How can you apply Isaiah 41:10 to your life? Most importantly, what will you're Prayer be?

Day Nine

Isaiah 58:11

"The Lord will guide you continually, giving you water when you are dry and restoring your strength. You will be like a well-watered garden, like an ever-flowing spring."

How great is the Father's love for us!

Countless times it is written how He will never forsake us! In our valley of death, when our souls are heavy with burden, He is with us! Gently guiding our weary souls to his place of comfort.

As Elijah wanted to die, God sent an angel to take care of him.

When Shadrach, Meshach, and Abednego refused to worship King Nebuchadnezzar, God sent an angel to protect them from the roaring flames.

When Daniel was thrown into the lion's den, God protected him.

Not only will God protect us but He will nourish our souls and body with what we need.

When our souls become weary, we can rest in the promise that He will take care of us. After all, as Jesus states in *John 6:35:*

"I am the bread of life..."

What did you observe? How can you apply Isaiah 58:11 to your life? Most importantly, what will you're Prayer be?

Day Ten

Ecclesiastes 3:1□-□12

"For everything, there is a season, a time for every activity under heaven.□□□□□□□□

A time to be born and a time to die.

A time to plant and a time to harvest.

A time to kill and a time to heal.

A time to tear down and a time to build up. A time to cry and a time to laugh.

A time to grieve and a time to dance.

A time to scatter stones and a time to gather stones.

A time to embrace and a time to turn away.

A time to search and a time to quit searching.

A time to keep and a time to throw away. A time to tear and a time to mend.

A time to be quiet and a time to speak.

A time to love and a time to hate.

A time for war and a time for peace.

What do people really get for all their hard work? I have seen the burden God has placed on us all. Yet God has made everything beautiful for its own time.

He has planted eternity in the human heart, but even so, people cannot see the whole scope of God's work from beginning to end. So I concluded there is nothing better than to be happy and enjoy ourselves as long as we can."

There is a time for everything.

We foolishly believe that we have control, especially over things that are impossible to control.

"... yet God has made everything beautiful for its own time..."

Life and our very existence were designed by the one who created the universe.

Before we were conceived, God knew our story and how it would end.

When I felt alone, this verse challenged me to think otherwise. Life was designed in perfect detail, and there were no mistakes made by Him. In *Ecclesiastes 3:1-12,* Solomon writes that God set eternity in our hearts-how wonderful is that?

As a result of this, we know that there is more out there, than this world.

Our time of weeping will turn into laughter and our time of mourning will turn into dance.

Just hang on, you're time is coming!

What did you observe? How can you apply Ecclesiastes 3:1-12 to your life? Most importantly, what will you're Prayer be?

Bonus Chapter

Genesis 30:22-24

Rachel

Then God remembered Rachel's plight and answered her prayers by enabling her to have children. She became pregnant and gave birth to a son.

"God has removed my disgrace," she said. And she named him Joseph, for she said, "May the Lord add yet another son to my family."

Day Eleven

James 5:13-15

"Are any of you suffering hardships? You should pray.

Are any of you happy? You should sing praises.

Are any of you sick? You should call for the elders of the church to come and pray over you, anointing you with oil in the name of the Lord.

Such a prayer offered in faith will heal the sick, and the Lord will make you well. And if you have committed any sins, you will be forgiven."

No matter the circumstance, *pray.*

When words escape your mouth, the Holy Spirit will intercede on your behalf. You just have to open your heart to God. Give Him the opportunity to work miracles in your life.

There were times where I felt guilty praying. Selfish even, but as I continued to relentlessly seek after God and pray, I realized over the course of my journey my relationship had grown stronger with God.

Remember, at some point in our relationship with the Lord, that we were once like the prodigal son. As he ran to the father whose arms were wide open, so is our Father in heaven. He wants us to run to him with our troubles.

What did you observe? How can you apply James 5:13-15 to your life? Most importantly, what will you're Prayer be?

Day Twelve

Psalm 9:2

"I will be filled with joy because of you. I will sing praises to your name, O Most High."

Gradually as you give your troubles to God, you'll begin to realize that the good days outweigh the bad.

Your once anxious heart will beat with a steady rhythm.

Of course, we're going to have bad days but as we grow in Christ, so will our joy.

We're told to not dwell in the past but to look toward the future and finish the race. How could we not be filled with joy, if we set our eyes on what is above and on the promises that await us?

Knowing what awaits me at the end of my journey has given me so much peace and joy. Why wouldn't I sing praises to the God who loves me? To Jesus who saved me?

As *Matthew 6:21* declares: *"Where your treasure is, there your heart will be also."*

What did you observe? How can you apply Psalm 9:2 to your life? Most importantly, what will you're Prayer be?

Day Thirteen

Job 37:5

"He does great things beyond our understanding. "

After my miscarriage, there was so much confusion. What was the point in getting pregnant, just to lose the baby?

Countless times, I prayed for understanding but it wasn't until I truly gave myself to God that I understood. As I continued to heal and seek God's word, I realized what I wanted in life had completely changed.

By my miscarriage, God was working through me to help others!

The faith that I had as a child was slowly returning to me, my broken heart was suddenly on fire to help other hurting mommies out there find their way back to God.

Ask God to reveal what He is doing in your life!

What did you observe? How can you apply Job 37:5 to your life? Most importantly, what will you're Prayer be?

Day Fourteen

Matthew 11:28-30

"Then Jesus said, "Come to me, all of you who are weary and carry heavy burdens, and I will give you rest."

There were days when I tried so hard to push through the pain and then later the anxiety.

I thought I had to be strong on my own. Every second of the day was spent trying to stay busy so that I didn't have to think or feel.

Right after we had lost the baby, my husband made a small flower bed in dedication; surrounded by rocks, bits of moss, and two small angel figurines in the middle of the bed.

It meant the world to me! I remember watching my husband filling the flower bed with the dirt and feeling blessed beyond measure, I thank God everyday for him!

In late September, the bed was covered in fallen leaves.

I went out there with the intention of cleaning it up. Instead, my husband finds me in the bed, covered in dirt and tears. It was nearly October and my baby was supposed to be here on November 27th.

It felt as though my world was falling apart all over again.

At some point, my husband wraps me up in his arms, wiping away the tears from my eyes while his were filled with sadness.

"You have to give it all to God," He whispered.

I knew he was right, but how could I? My husband never let go, he held on tight- just as God was doing.

That night, I prayed. Laying everything at the Lord's feet because whatever strength was left was not enough to hold me up anymore.

In order to live and find peace, you *have to* give it to the Lord. We were not meant to live this life without God and his providence.

What did you observe? How can you apply Matthew 11:28-30 to your life? Most importantly, what will you're Prayer be?

Day Fifteen

Psalm 40:1-3

"I waited patiently for the Lord to help me, and he turned to me and heard my cry.

He lifted me out of the pit of despair, out of the mud and the mire.

He set my feet on solid ground and steadied me as I walked along.

He has given me a new song to sing, a hymn of praise to our God. Many will see what he has done and be amazed. They will put their trust in the Lord."

During difficult times, we are asked *over and over* to wait on the Lord and to have faith in his timing. However, in that moment when our emotions are high, we want the answers right then and there. But as the biblical Christians waited for deliverance- we too, must wait.

Ecclesiastes 3:11 reminds us that everything has its time.

God *will* reach down and rescue you from your pain, your anxiety, and your depression.

Just keep *hanging on.*

Just as Jesus saved us by dying on the cross; so will God rescue us from the mud and mire.

What did you observe? How can you apply Psalm 40:1-3 to your life? Most importantly, what will you're Prayer be?

Bonus Chapter

Samuel 1:1-20

Hannah

There was a man named Elkanah who lived in Ramah in the region of Zuph in the hill country of Ephraim.

He was the son of Jeroham, son of Elihu, son of Tohu, son of Zuph, of Ephraim. Elkanah had two wives, Hannah and Peninnah.

Peninnah had children, but Hannah did not. Each year Elkanah would travel to Shiloh to worship and sacrifice to the Lord of Heaven's Armies at the Tabernacle. The priests of the Lord at that time were the two sons of Eli—Hophni and Phinehas. On the days Elkanah presented his sacrifice, he would give portions of the meat to Peninnah and each of her children. And though he loved Hannah, he would give her only one choice portion because the Lord had given her no children.

So Peninnah would taunt Hannah and make fun of her because the Lord had kept her from having children. Year after year it was the same—Peninnah would taunt Hannah as they went to the Tabernacle. Each time, Hannah would be reduced to tears and would not even eat.

"Why are you crying, Hannah?" Elkanah would ask. "Why aren't you eating? Why be downhearted just because you have no children? You have me—isn't that better than having ten sons?"

Once after a sacrificial meal at Shiloh, Hannah got up and went to pray. Eli the priest was sitting at his customary place beside the entrance of the Tabernacle. Hannah was in deep anguish, crying bitterly as she prayed to the Lord.

And she made this vow: "O Lord of Heaven's Armies, if you will look upon my sorrow and answer my prayer and give me a son, then I will give him back to you. He will be yours for his entire lifetime, and as a sign that he has been dedicated to the Lord, his hair will never be cut."

As she was praying to the Lord, Eli watched her. Seeing her lips moving but hearing no sound, he thought she had been drinking.

"Must you come here drunk?" he demanded. "Throw away your wine!"

"Oh no, sir!" she replied. "I haven't been drinking wine or anything stronger. But I am very discouraged, and I was pouring out my heart to the Lord. Don't think I am a wicked woman! For I have been praying out of great anguish and sorrow."

"In that case," Eli said, "go in peace! May the God of Israel grant the request you have asked of him."

"Oh, thank you, sir!" she exclaimed. Then she went back and began to eat again, and she was no longer sad. The entire family got up early the next morning and went to worship the Lord once more. Then they returned home to Ramah. When Elkanah slept with Hannah, the Lord remembered her plea, and in due time she gave birth to a son. She named him Samuel, for she said, "I asked the Lord for him."

Day Sixteen

Luke 8:43-48

"A woman in the crowd had suffered for twelve years with constant bleeding, and she could find no cure.

Coming up behind Jesus, she touched the fringe of his robe. Immediately, the bleeding stopped.

"Who touched me?" Jesus asked. Everyone denied it, and Peter said, "Master, this whole crowd is pressing up against you."

But Jesus said, "Someone deliberately touched me, for I felt healing power go out from me."

When the woman realized that she could not stay hidden, she began to tremble and fell to her knees in front of him. The whole crowd heard her explain why she had touched him and that she had been immediately healed.

"Daughter," he said to her, "your faith has made you well. Go in peace."

In *Psalm 40:1-3*, Daniel waited patiently for the Lord. It's no different in Luke when the woman who bled for twelve years was finally healed.

Sometimes God calls us to patiently wait on him, whether it be days, weeks, months, or years.

In that moment we may feel forgotten but the whole time God is carrying us, waiting for the perfect moment to deliver us. As a society that demands instant gratification, we must lean not on our own understanding but His. We must learn how to be patient.

This woman who searched for a cure, who was ostracized from her family, friends, and synagogues for twelve years never gave up. She touched the hem of Jesus' robe and was instantly healed.

How can you find rest in the Lord? How can you find patience in the midst of the storm?

What did you observe? How can you apply Luke 8:43-48 to your life? Most importantly, what will you're Prayer be?

Day Seventeen

Galatians 5:22-23

"But the Holy Spirit produces this kind of fruit in our lives: love, joy, peace, patience, kindness, goodness, faithfulness, gentleness, and self-control. There is no law against these things!"

As I started to heal, I was motivated more than ever to seek God in all aspects of my life.

Each day, I prayed asking Him to fill me with the Holy Spirit *(Romans 15:13)*. Eventually there was a shift in my spirit and the world was abruptly brighter. The fruit of the Holy Spirit is: *love, joy, peace, patience, kindness, goodness, faithfulness, gentleness, and self-control.*

All these things had started to take root and I was finally at peace with myself and what the future could hold.

The fear that had seized my heart was no longer there; instead, it was the fruit of God's goodness that was filling me.

If you haven't already, why don't you pray right now for the Holy Spirit to fill you? Maybe start a 30-day challenge, where you pray for a clean heart and to be filled with the Holy Ghost? Pray for the same thing to happen to your husband; or, better yet, pray for it together.

When you give all of your pain to the Lord, you are going to find rest. When you find rest, joy will soon follow after.

What did you observe? How can you apply Galatians 5:22-23 to your life? Most importantly, what will you're Prayer be?

Day Eighteen

Psalm 4:7-8

"You have given me greater joy than those who have abundant harvests of grain and new wine. In peace I will lie down and sleep, for you alone, O Lord, will keep me safe."

Once you give yourself to God, there will be a radical shift in your soul.

Truly, you will be filled with joy because you *know* what His promises are. You know at the end of your journey He's going to call you home. Life will continue on- and there will be days where we are going to struggle; but, we can take heart and know that Jesus has already conquered the world.

How could we not be filled with joy, knowing this? How could we not feel at peace? The Lord of the universe loves *you!*

So, remain joyful in hope, patient in affliction, and faithful in prayer. *(Romans: 12:12).*

What did you observe? How can you apply Psalm 4:7-8 to your life? Most importantly, what will you're Prayer be?

Day Nineteen

Daniel 3:16-18

Shadrach, Meshach, and Abednego replied, "O Nebuchadnezzar, we do not need to defend ourselves before you.

If we are thrown into the blazing furnace, the God whom we serve is able to save us. He will rescue us from your power, Your Majesty.

But even if he doesn't, we want to make it clear to you, Your Majesty, that we will never serve your gods or worship the gold statue you have set up."

In the book of *Daniel,* Shadrach, Meshach, and Abednego were facing death because of their unwavering faith in the Lord. They knew that God would rescue them. However, they included: *"But even if he doesn't, we want to make it clear to you, Your Majesty, that we will never serve your gods or worship the gold statue you have set up."*

Even if they weren't rescued, these men knew that the Lord still loved them and He was still a good and faithful Father.

Do you remember in *Ecclesiastes 3:11* that everything has a time? God knew us before we were formed in our mother's womb; He calls us by name and knows our story. God hears us when we cry out to Him.

Sometimes what we want and what God wants are two completely different things.

Even if I don't conceive again, I am filled with peace with two things:

1. I have conceived and my baby is with the Lord. One day, we will be reunited.

2. God's love is everlasting. He has shown me love when I couldn't love myself, forgiven and protected me. Knowing that I would backslide... He never gave up on me.

Over and over God urges us to give every piece of ourselves to Him, Jesus died on the cross so that we may live and have a relationship with his Father. Relentlessly, we are pursued, and we are given promises that are not meant for this world. So, yes, *even if* I am still going to praise the Lord.

I will still love Him.

I will still follow Him.

What did you observe? How can you apply Daniel 3:16-18 to your life? Most importantly, what will you're Prayer be?

Day Twenty

Psalm 139:1-18

"O Lord, you have examined my heart and know everything about me.

You know when I sit down or stand up. You know my thoughts even when I'm far away.

You see me when I travel and when I rest at home.

You know everything I do. You know what I am going to say even before I say it, Lord.

You go before me and follow me. You place your hand of blessing on my head. Such knowledge is too wonderful for me, too great for me to understand!

I can never escape from your Spirit! I can never get away from your presence! If I go up to heaven, you are there; if I go down to the grave, you are there.

If I ride the wings of the morning, if I dwell by the farthest oceans, even there your hand will guide me, and your strength will support me. I could ask the darkness to hide me and the light around me to become night— but even in darkness, I cannot hide from you.

To you the night shines as bright as day. Darkness and light are the same to you. You made all the delicate, inner parts of my body and knit me together in my mother's womb. Thank you for making me so wonderfully complex! Your workmanship is marvelous—how well I know it. You watched me as I was being formed in utter seclusion, as I was woven together in the dark of the womb.

You saw me before I was born. Every day of my life was recorded in your book. Every moment was laid out before a single day had passed. How precious are your thoughts about me, O God. They cannot be numbered! I can't even count them; they outnumber the grains of sand! And when I wake up, you are still with me!"

As we close this Bible study, let's reflect on all the goodness God has given us.

The Lord of the universe, who calls me by name, knows my heart and everything about me. In the sea of people, I am not lost or forgotten. He walks before me and guides me with His righteous right hand.

When life becomes too much to bear and our faith becomes stagnant or crumbles, we know that no matter how far we stray, it is never too late to turn around and run back. No matter where life takes us in this fallen world, we can take comfort that God will never abandon us.

Life after loss is a journey that I will always keep in my heart. My baby will always be with me, just as your baby will always be with you.

At some point, we're going to experience grief again, or anxiety and depression- but we cannot let that define who we are in Christ.

We have to live a life worth living. Grow in your relationship with God, live a Proverbs 31 life, and continue running that race, we are all called to do.

If you're struggling with your faith, if you feel stuck, or maybe you haven't given yourself to Christ, please know that it's never too late. Open your heart and invite Jesus in. Pray for God's healing hand to touch your heart and to open your eyes.

Pray for peace.

Pray for forgiveness.

You're loved beyond measure, never forget that.

Dear Lord,

Please be with us as we go through this journey that we call life. Heal our hearts, Lord. Be with us and hold us close.

Lord, open our eyes so that we may see what you see. Open our ears so that we may hear what you hear. Dear God, please be with the women who is reading this; her heart is heavy and her soul is weak. Guide her, dear Lord, to your place of comfort.

Guide us always, with your righteous right hand.

In Jesus name, I pray.

Amen.

What did you observe? How can you apply Psalm 139:1-18 to your life? Most importantly, what will you're Prayer be?

Don't miss out!

Visit the website below and you can sign up to receive emails whenever Maria Davis publishes a new book. There's no charge and no obligation.

https://books2read.com/r/B-A-ASIBB-XIQQC

BOOKS 2 READ

Connecting independent readers to independent writers.

About the Author

Maria Davis is an author based out of Clinton, Arkansas, with two dogs, and a best friend for a husband. Maria often finds herself in the woods, where she is the most comfortable. With her stories, she hopes to spread God's word to those who need it the most.